# NATURE AND ANIMAL COLORING BOOK

## 100 COLORING IMAGES FOR ADULTS AND CHILDREN

EE-KAY

# Examples from the Interior

# Acknowledgments

Hello and THANK YOU so much for choosing our coloring book! We hope you enjoy it as much as we have enjoyed creating it. This book has been made with all the love in the world and contains a wide variety of images for adults, children, and anyone who wants to disconnect and escape from the world for a little while. From natural landscapes to abstract drawings, each of these images is filled with details and subtleties that will invite you to immerse yourself in the world of creativity and color.

We hope our book is a source of relaxation and fun for you and that you can enjoy hours and hours of coloring. If you liked our book, we kindly ask you to leave a comment that will help us reach other people and share our love for coloring. Thank you again for choosing our book and we hope you enjoy it very much!

# Benefits of Painting

Painting is a creative activity that can be very beneficial for our minds and well-being. For a long time, painting has been considered to have therapeutic properties and is capable of providing a number of benefits for the mind and body.

- As you begin to paint, you can feel your mind focusing on the present and clearing of all distractions. Painting allows you to set aside your thoughts and worries and focus on the here and now.

- You can feel your muscles relaxing and your breathing becoming deeper and more regular. Painting helps you to release the stress and tension accumulated in your body and feel more at peace and balanced.

- In addition, painting can also be a very rewarding way to express yourself and release your emotions. By choosing colors and creating shapes and patterns, you can express your feelings and thoughts in a very personal and unique way. This can be very liberating and help you feel more in tune with yourself and the world around you.

- If you are feeling stressed or anxious, or simply need a relaxing and rewarding activity, painting can be an excellent option. Encourage yourself to try it!

# Tips for Painting

Coloring can be a very fun and relaxing activity, and no special skills are needed to do it. However, there are some tricks and tips that can help you get the most out of your drawings and improve your coloring skills. Here are some simple instructions for painting a coloring book well:

- **Choose your tools:** for coloring, you can use colored pencils, markers, or even acrylic or watercolor paints. It's important to choose the right tools for the type of paper you have in your book, as some may be more or less absorbent than others.

- **Make sure you have enough light:** it's important to have enough light to see the details of your drawings and choose the right colors. If possible, work near a window or use a table lamp to illuminate your work area.

- **Use different shades and intensities:** to give depth and texture to your drawings, you can use different shades and intensities of color. For example, you can use a lighter shade for more distant areas or a darker shade for closer areas. You can also mix colors to create new shades.

- **Follow the lines:** it's important to follow the lines of the drawing when coloring, as this will help you maintain the symmetry and balance of your drawing. If you have trouble following the lines, you can use a pencil or a fine-tipped marker to mark them before coloring.

- **Practice:** coloring is an activity that is learned through practice. Don't worry if your drawings don't come out perfect at first, keep practicing and you will see how you improve gradually. Enjoy the process and don't focus too much on the final result!

I hope these instructions have been helpful and encourage you to try coloring. Remember that coloring is a very relaxing and rewarding activity, so don't feel pressured to do it well. **Enjoy the process of your colors and creativity!**

"Creativity is intelligence having fun."- Albert Einstein

Colors are a way to create beauty in your life. Use your colored pencils to add a little joy to your day

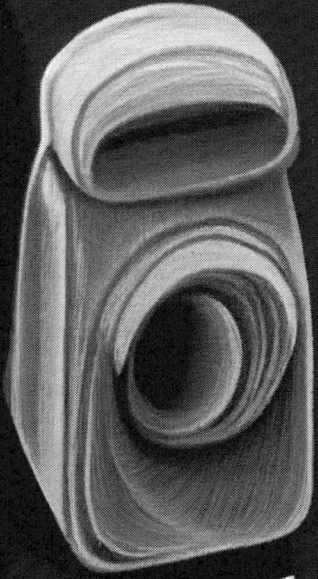

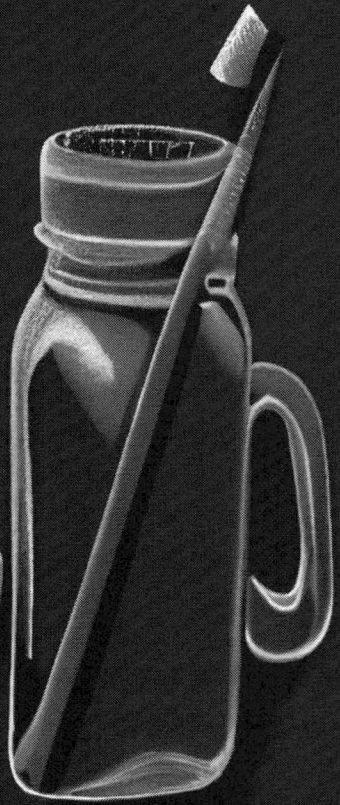

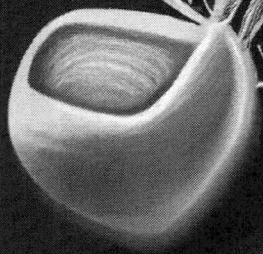

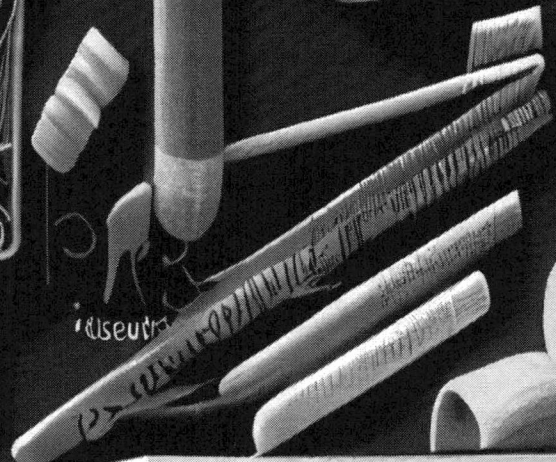

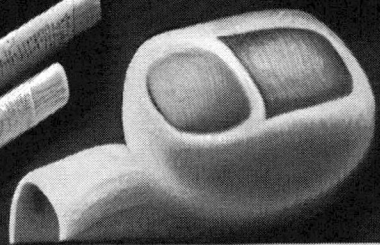

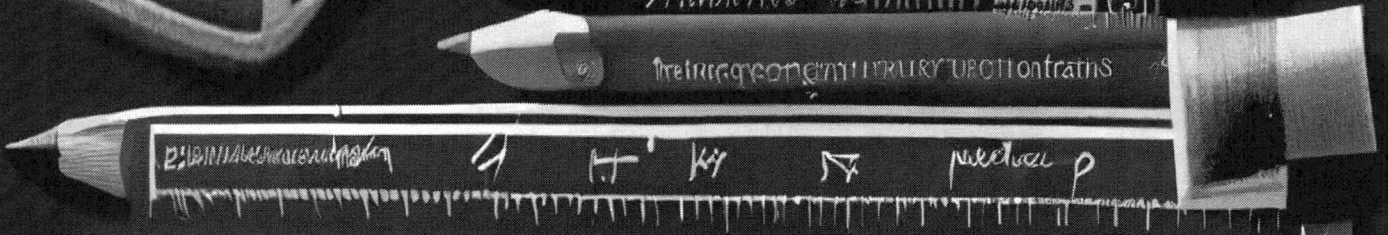

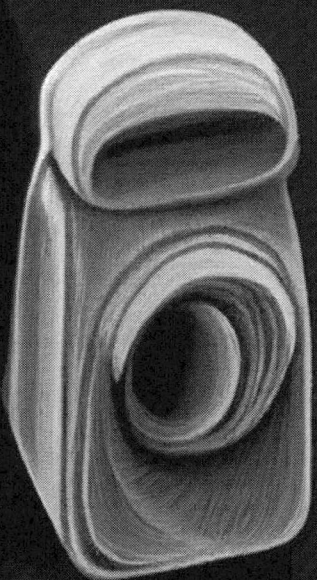

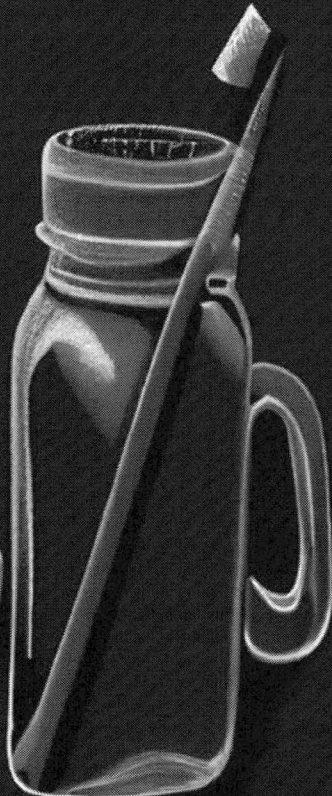

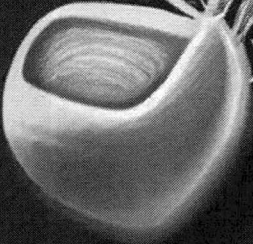

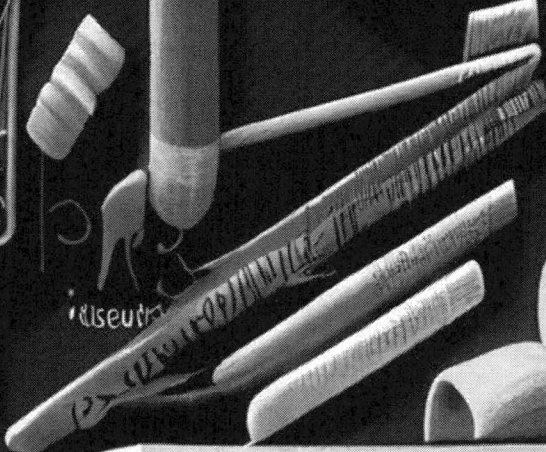

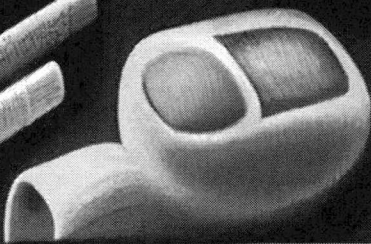

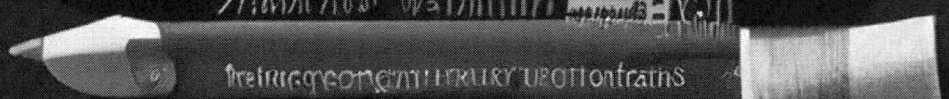

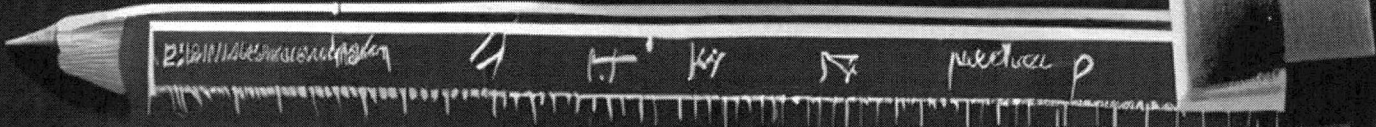

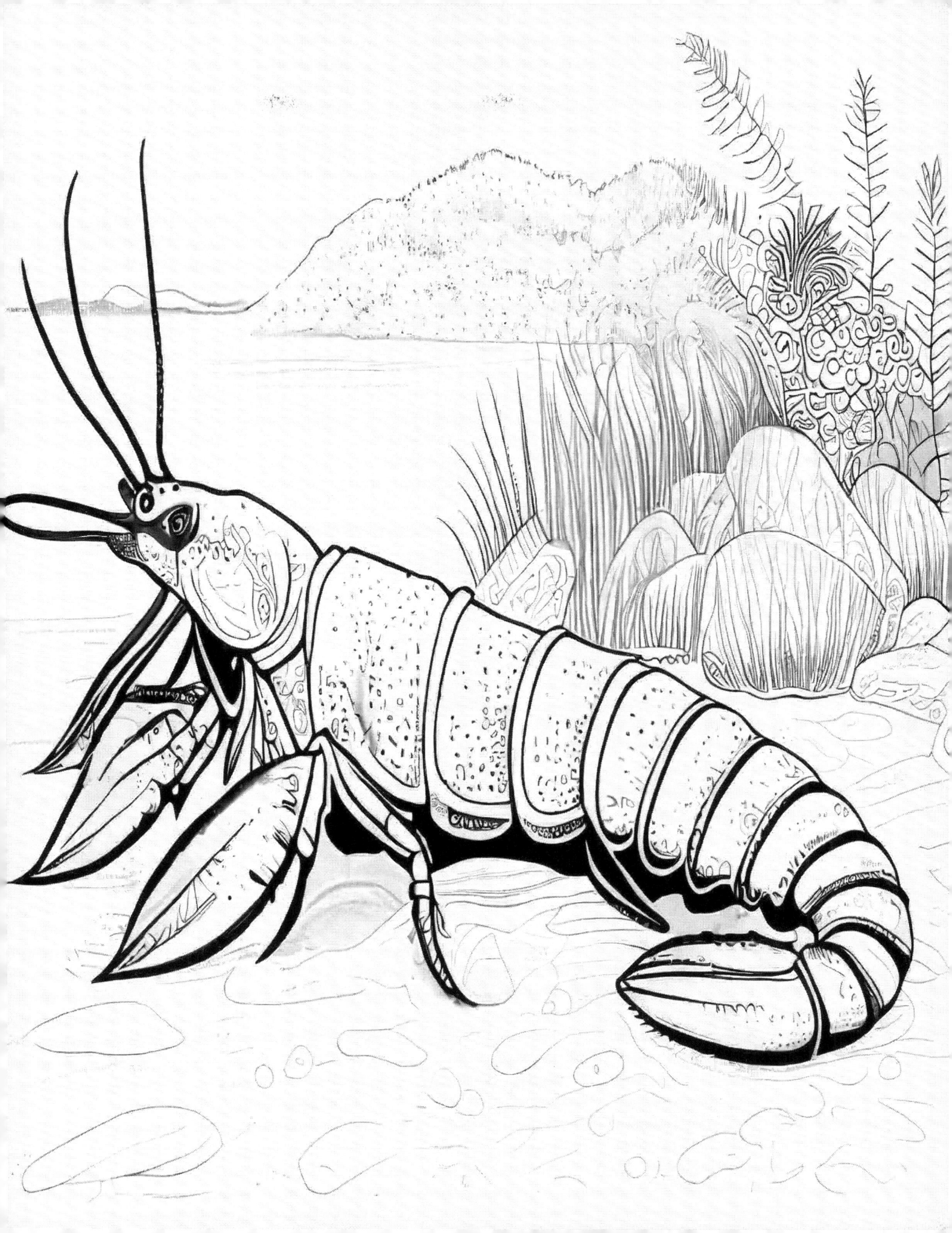

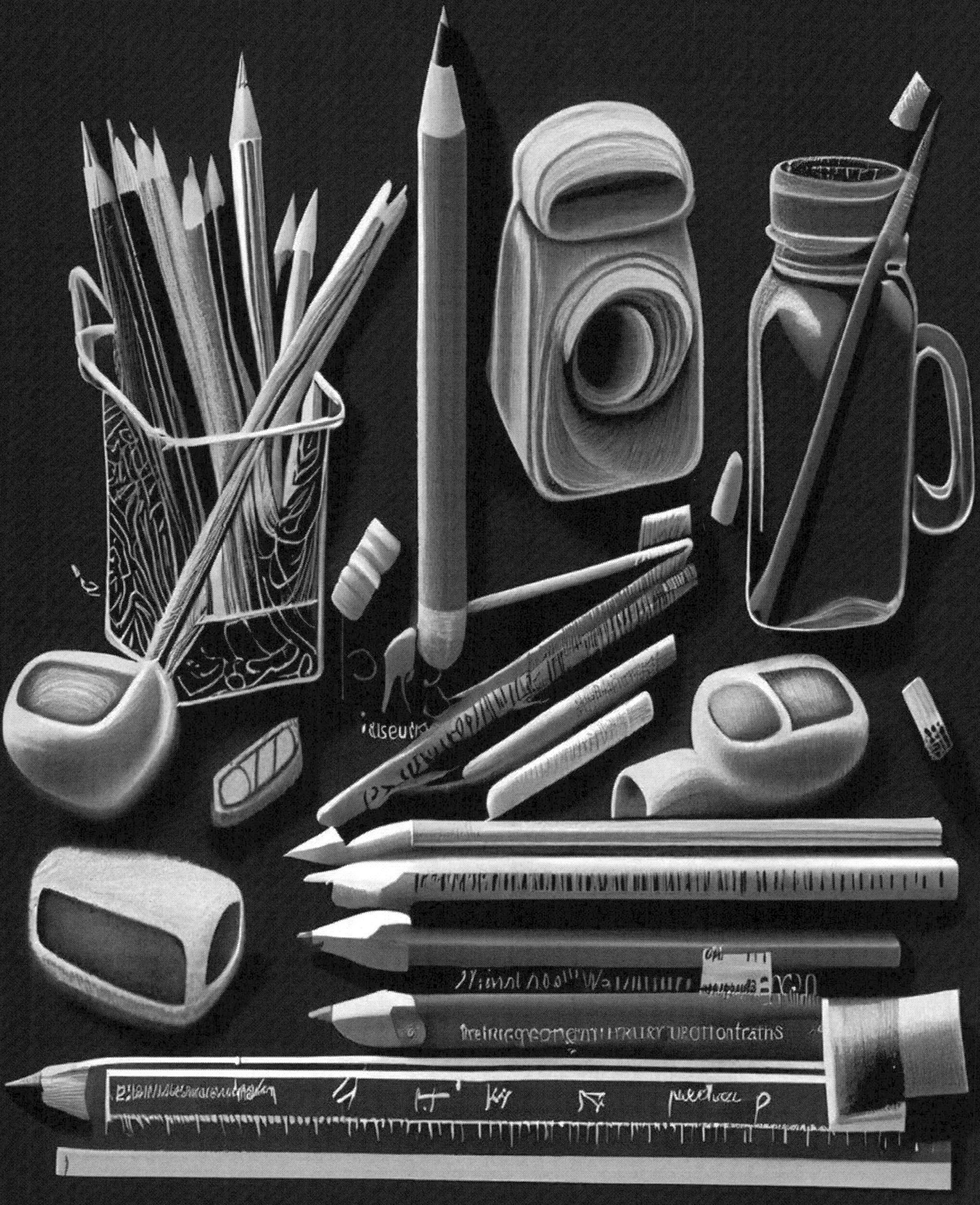

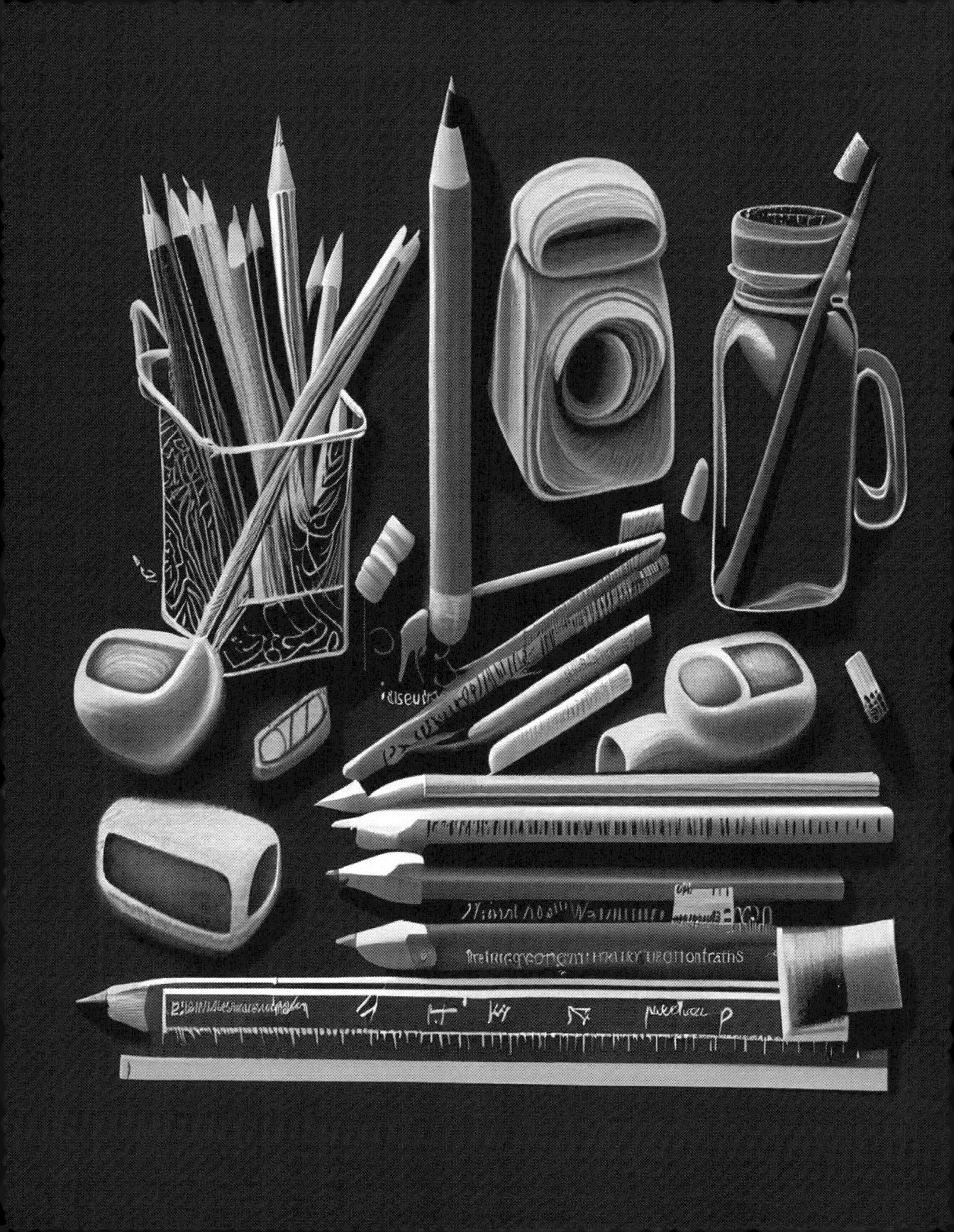

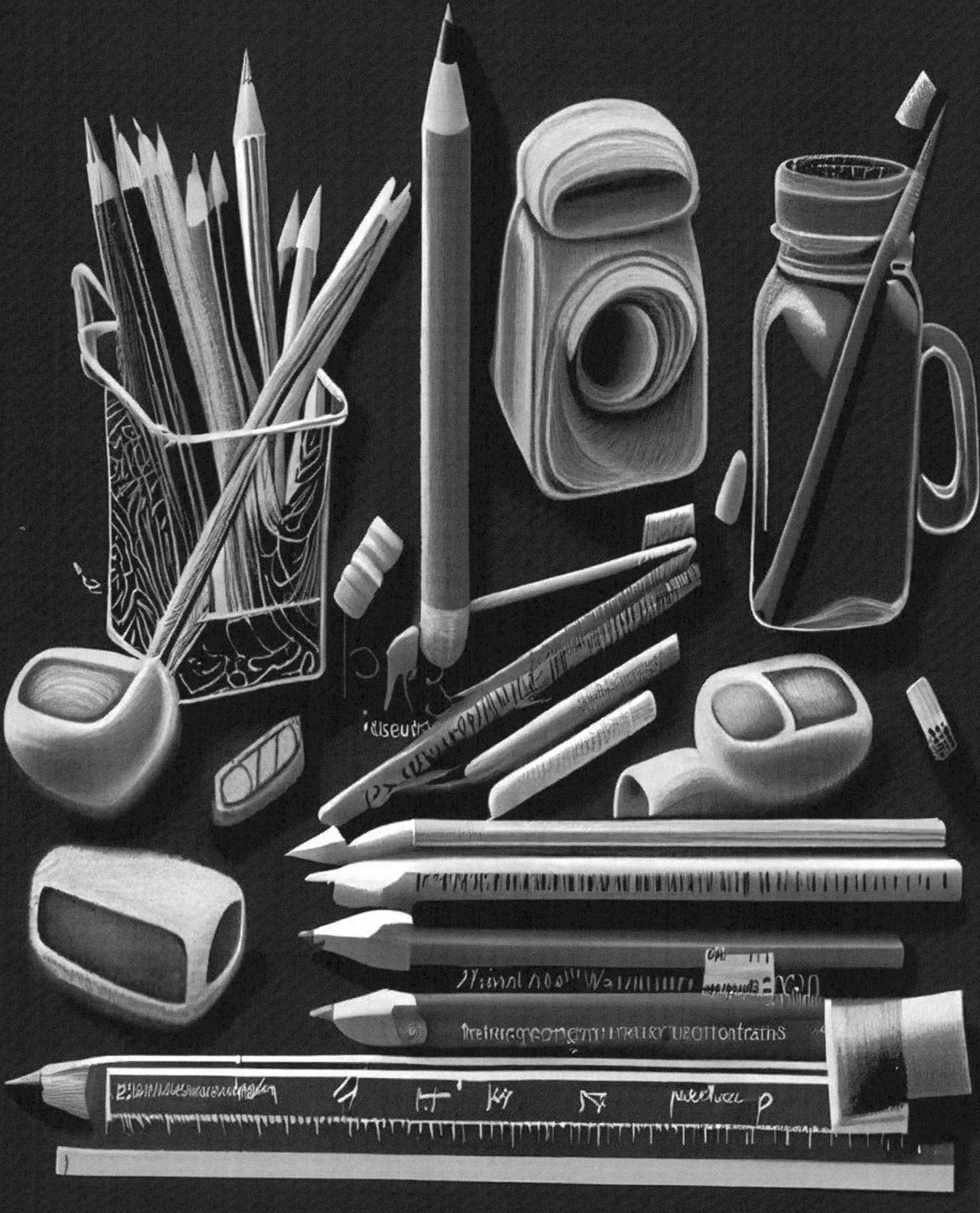

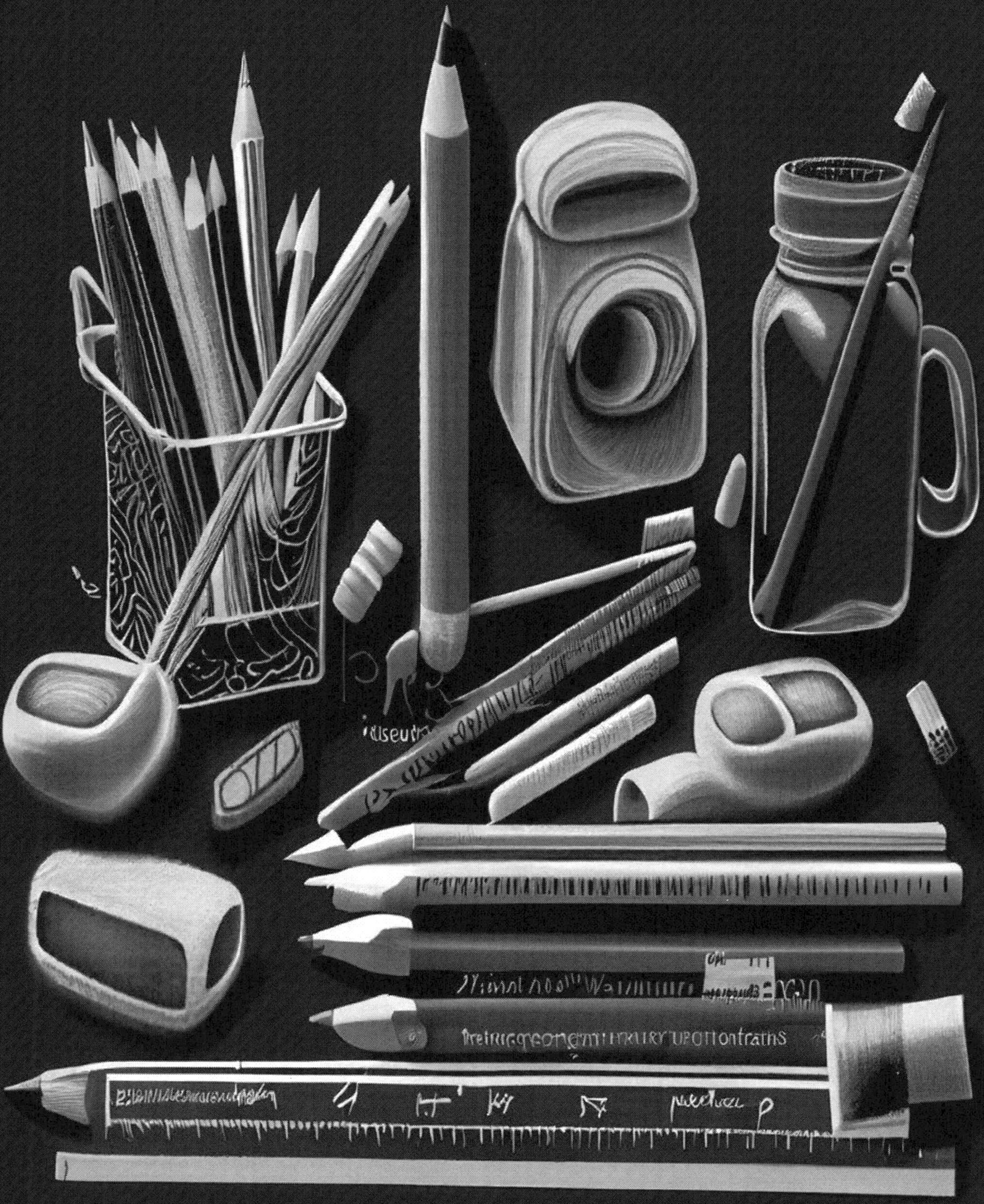

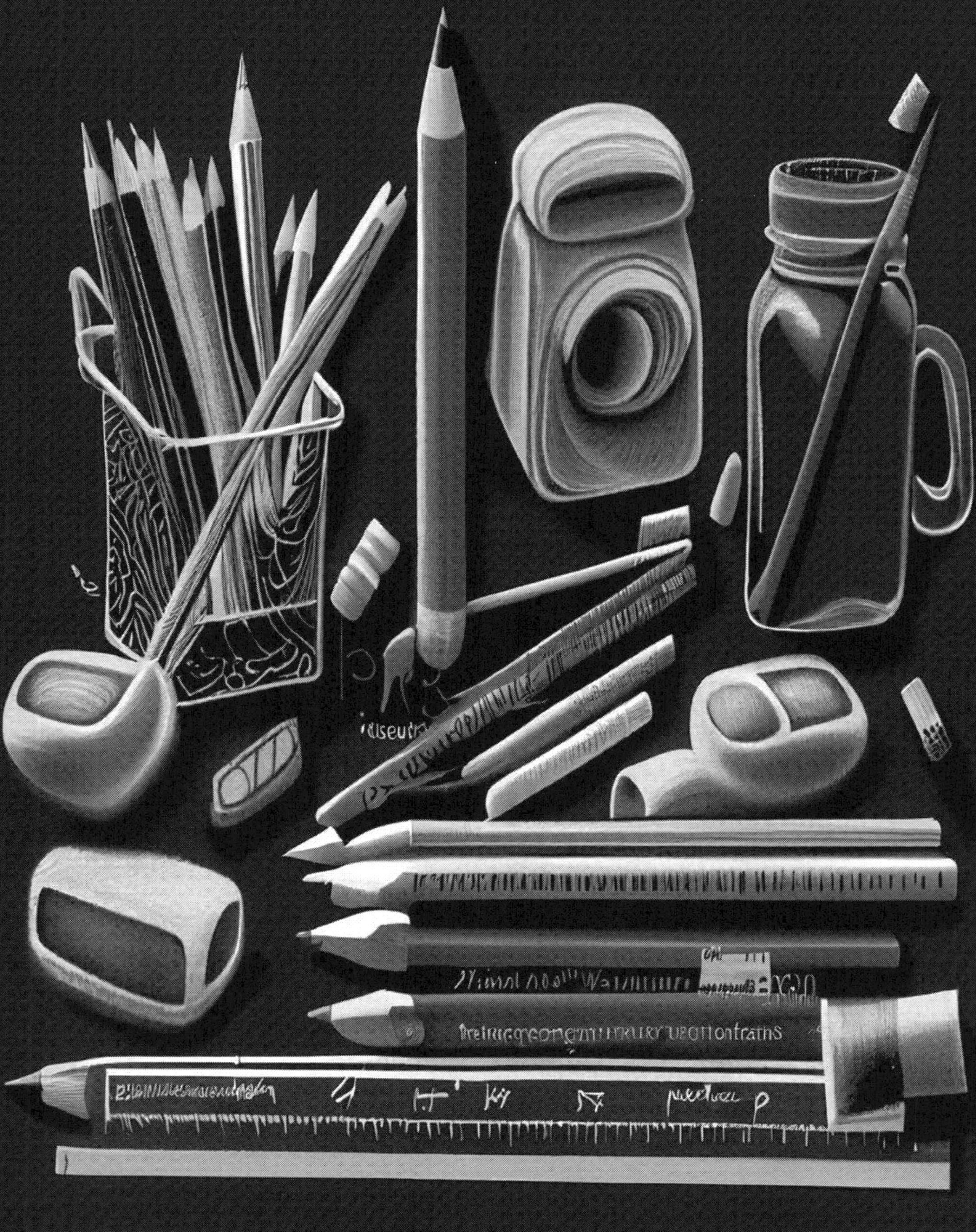

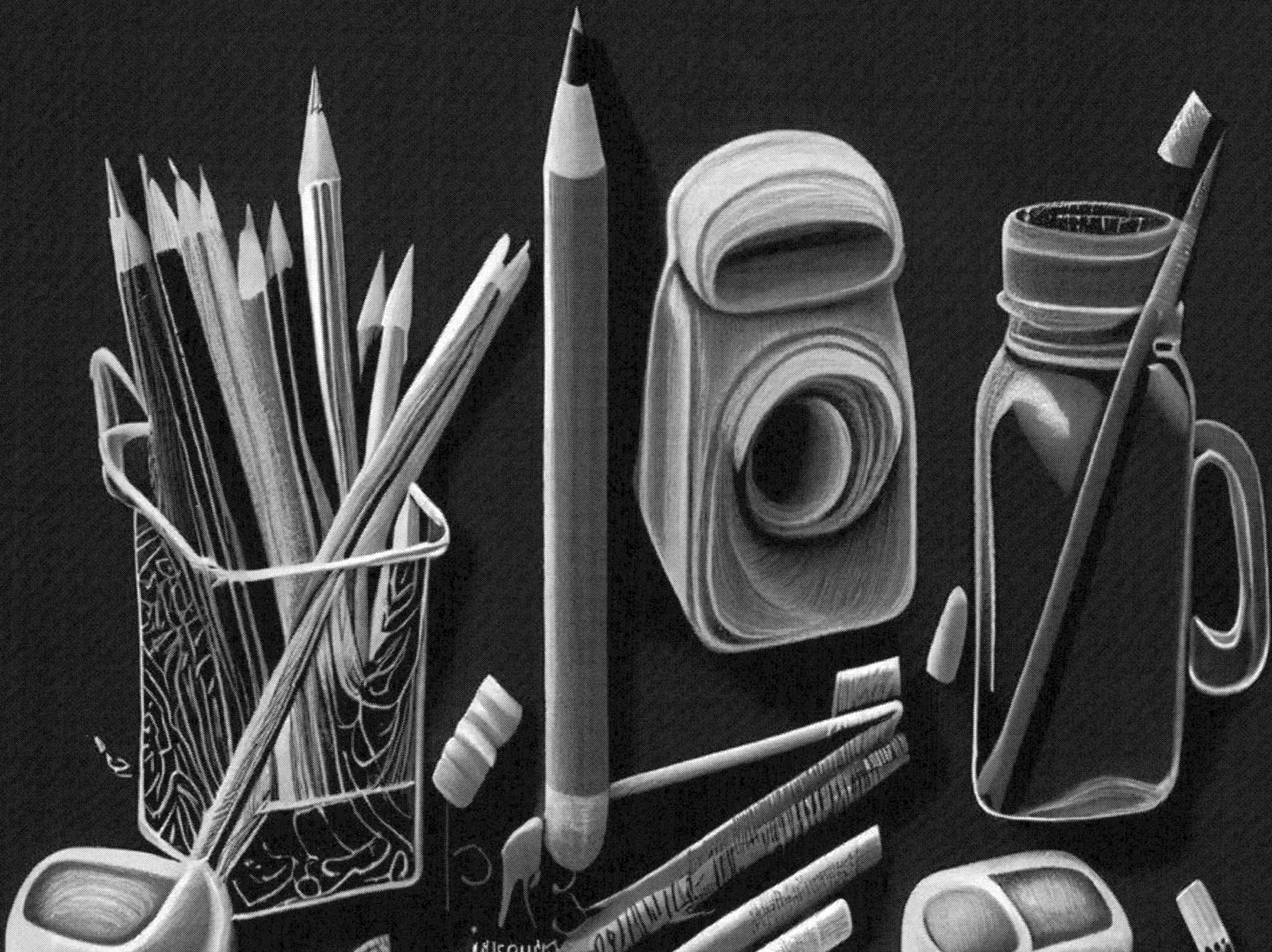

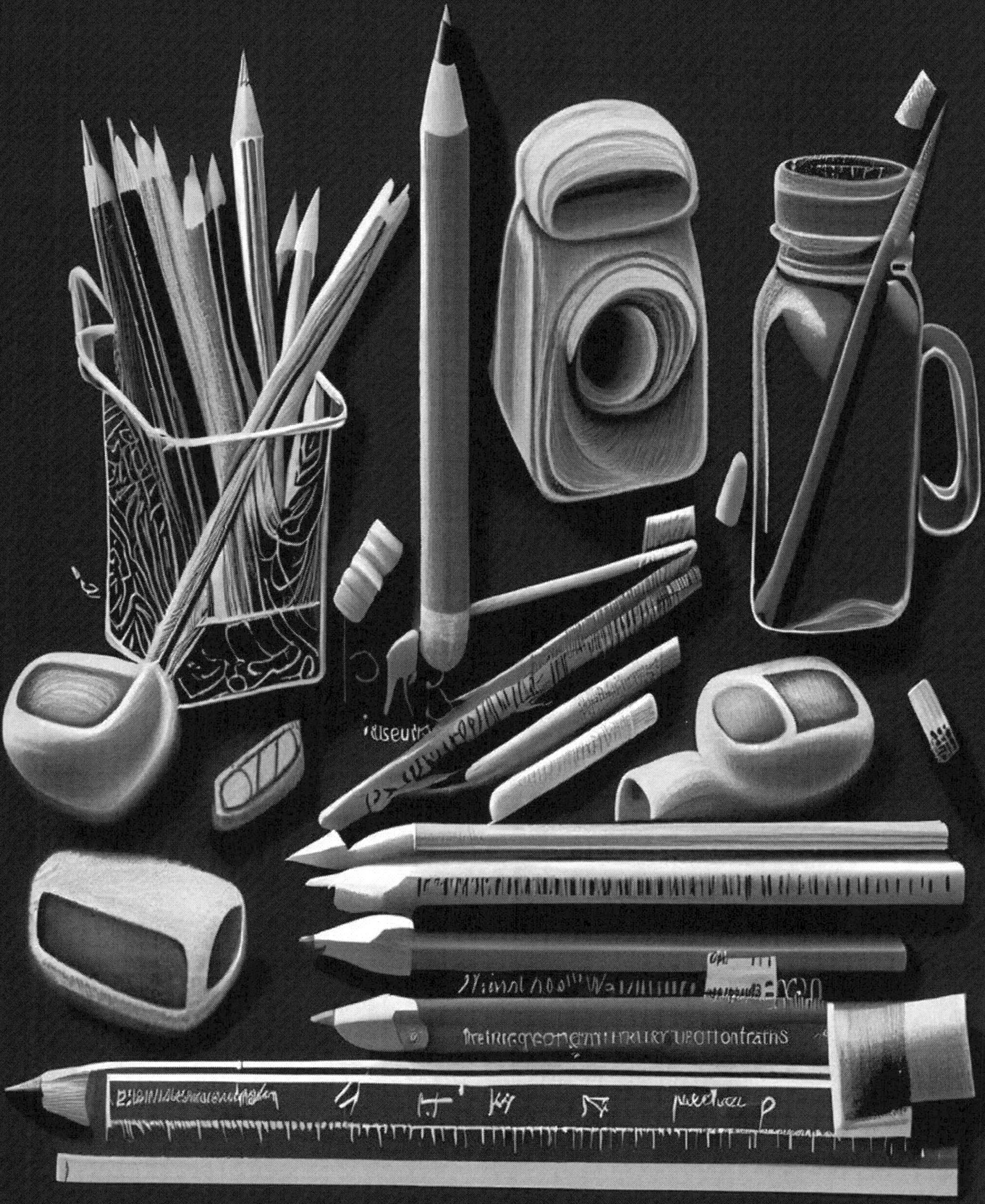

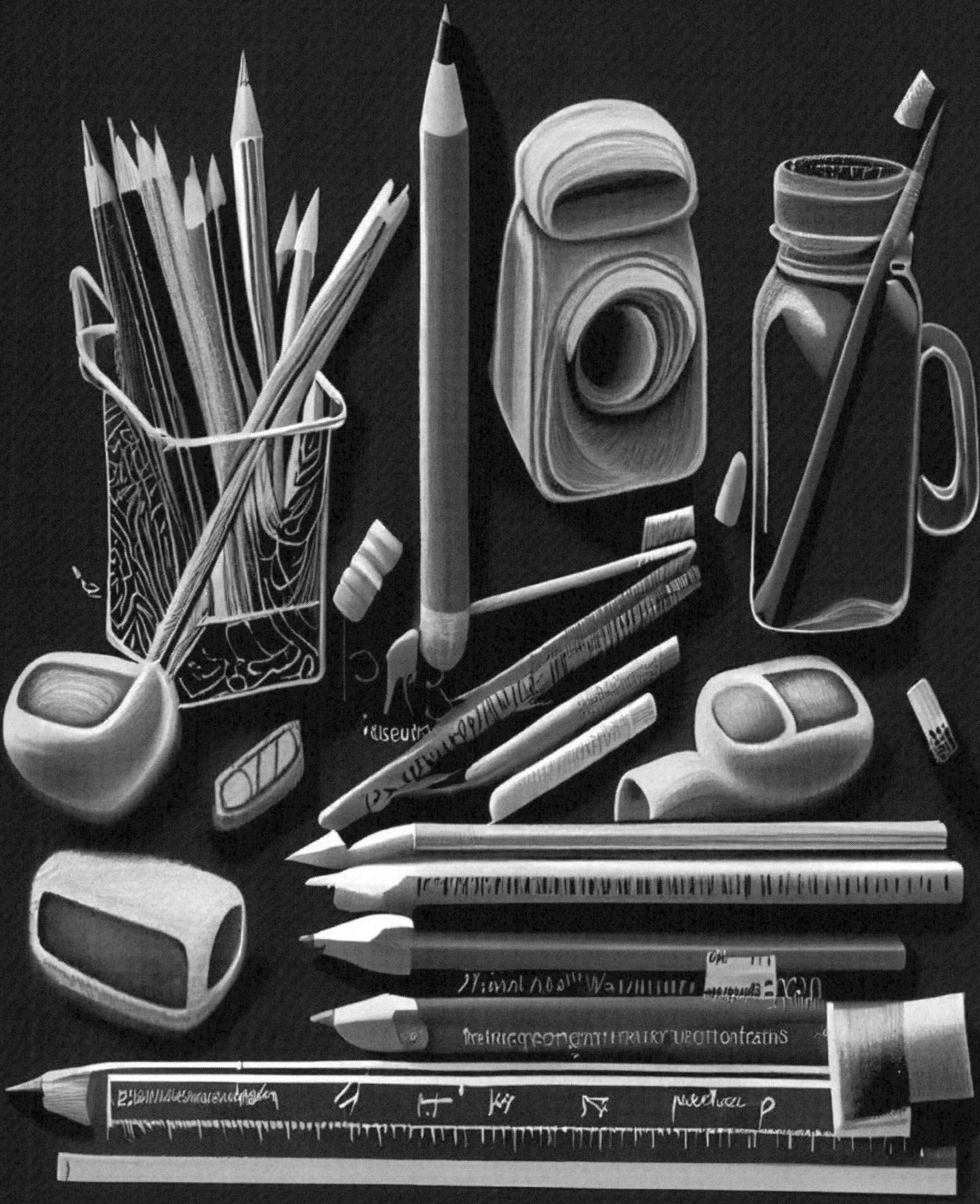

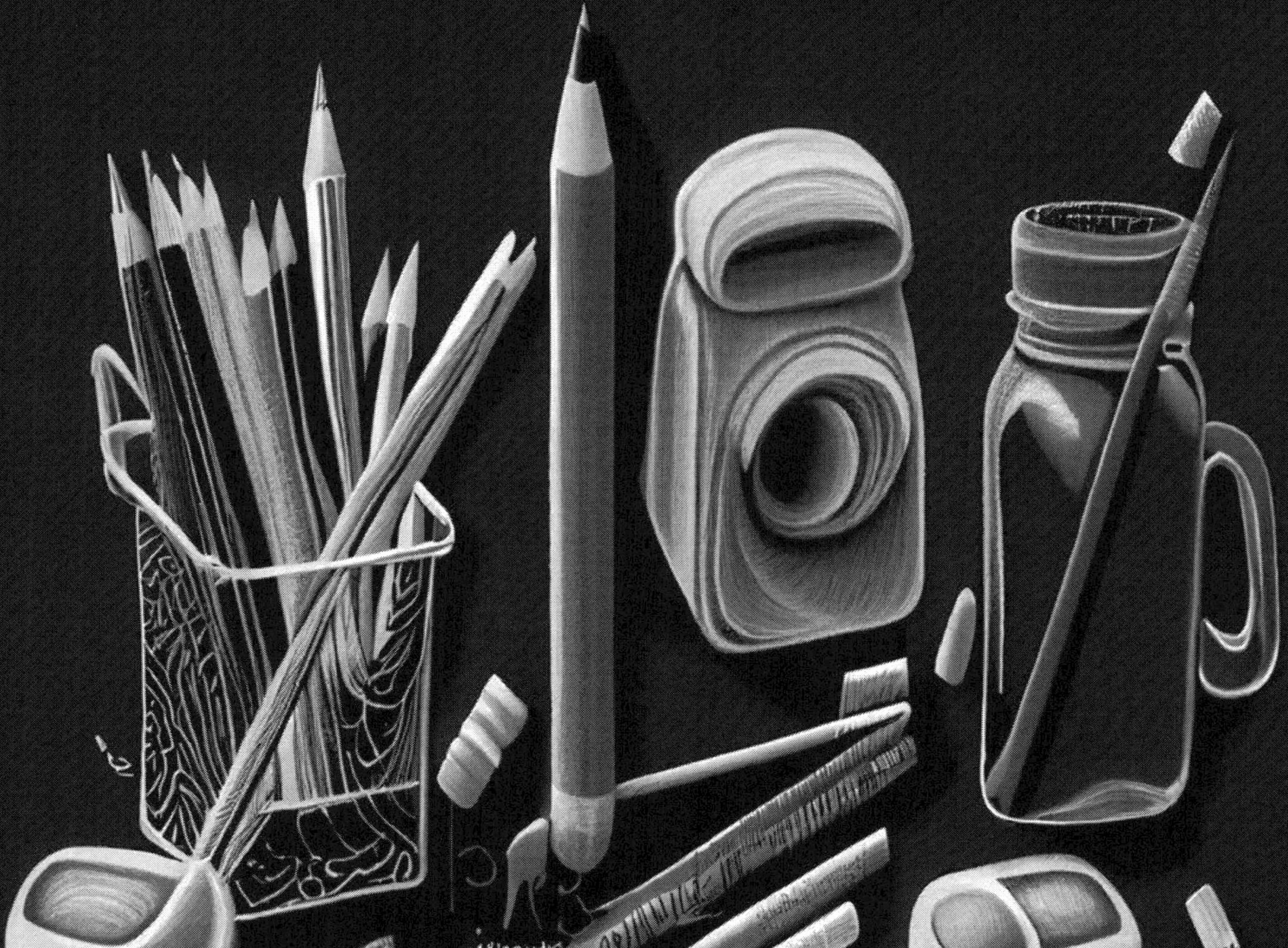

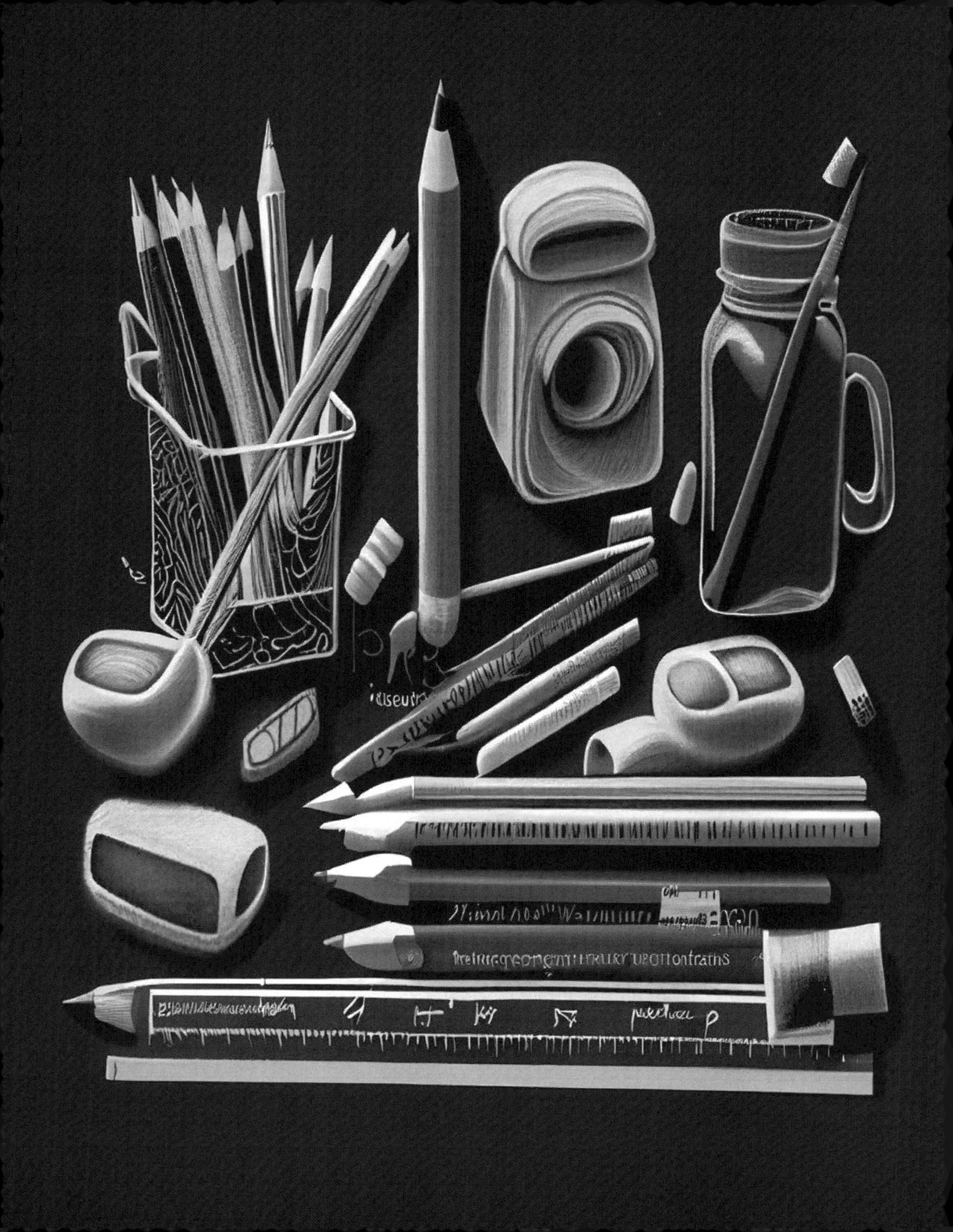

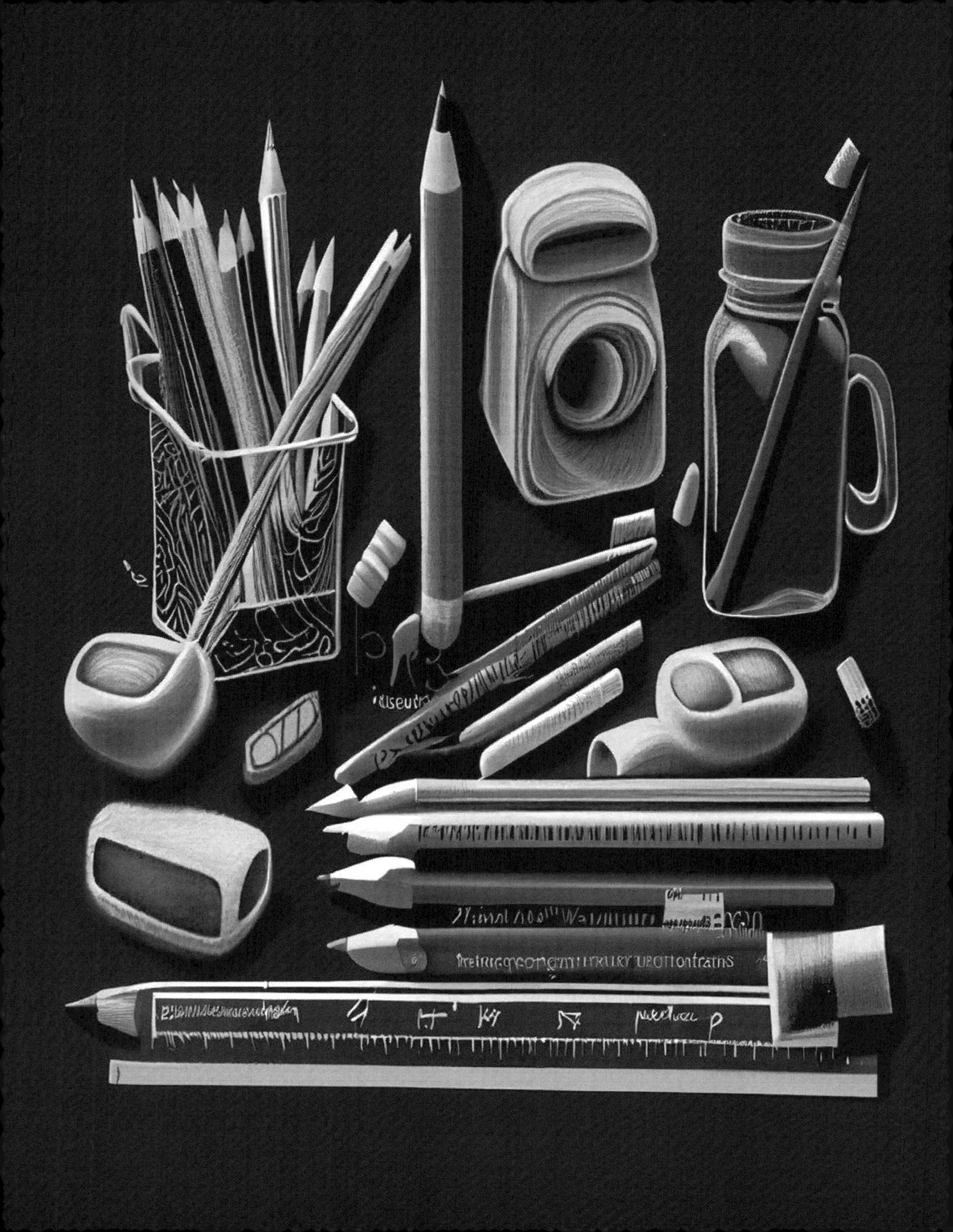

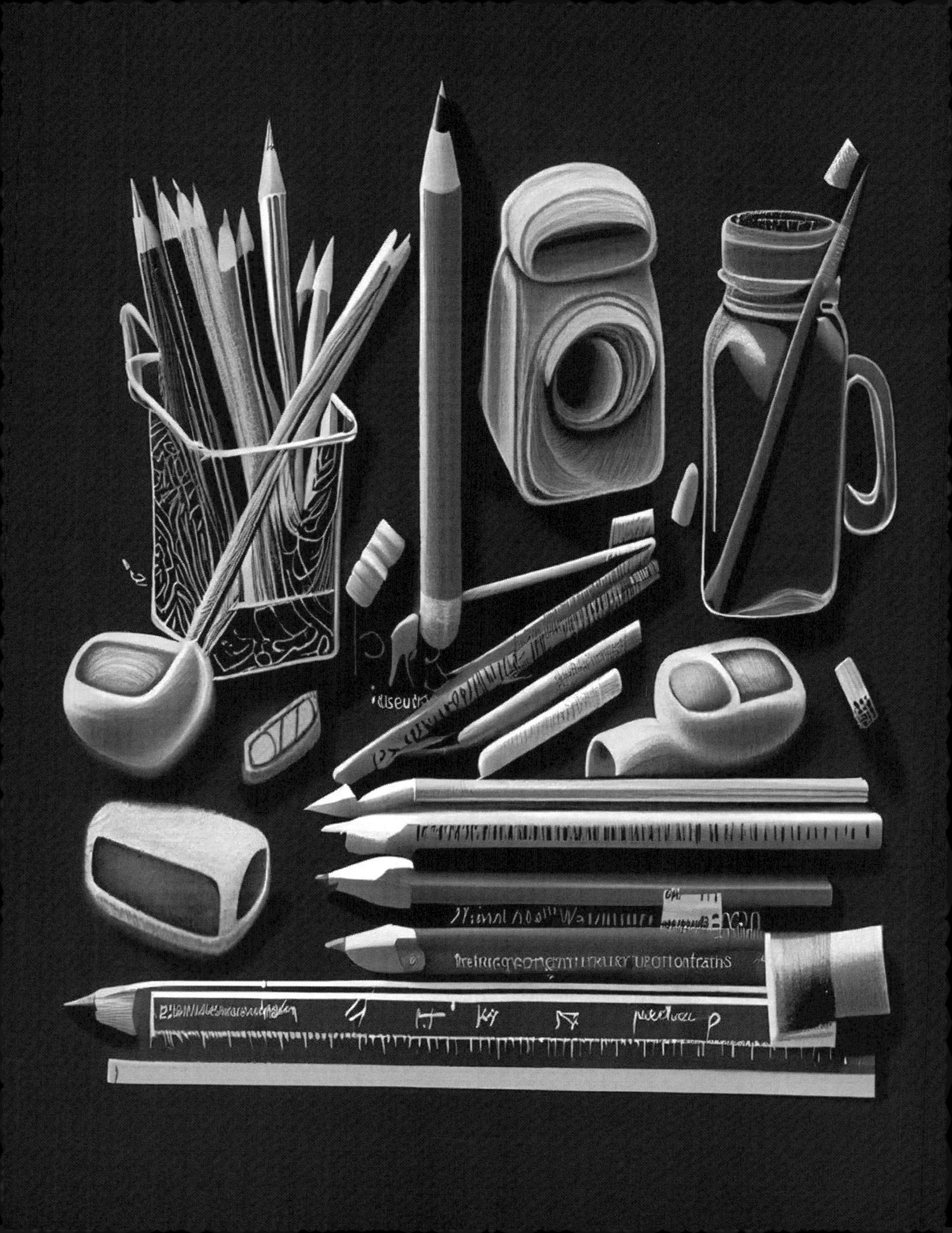

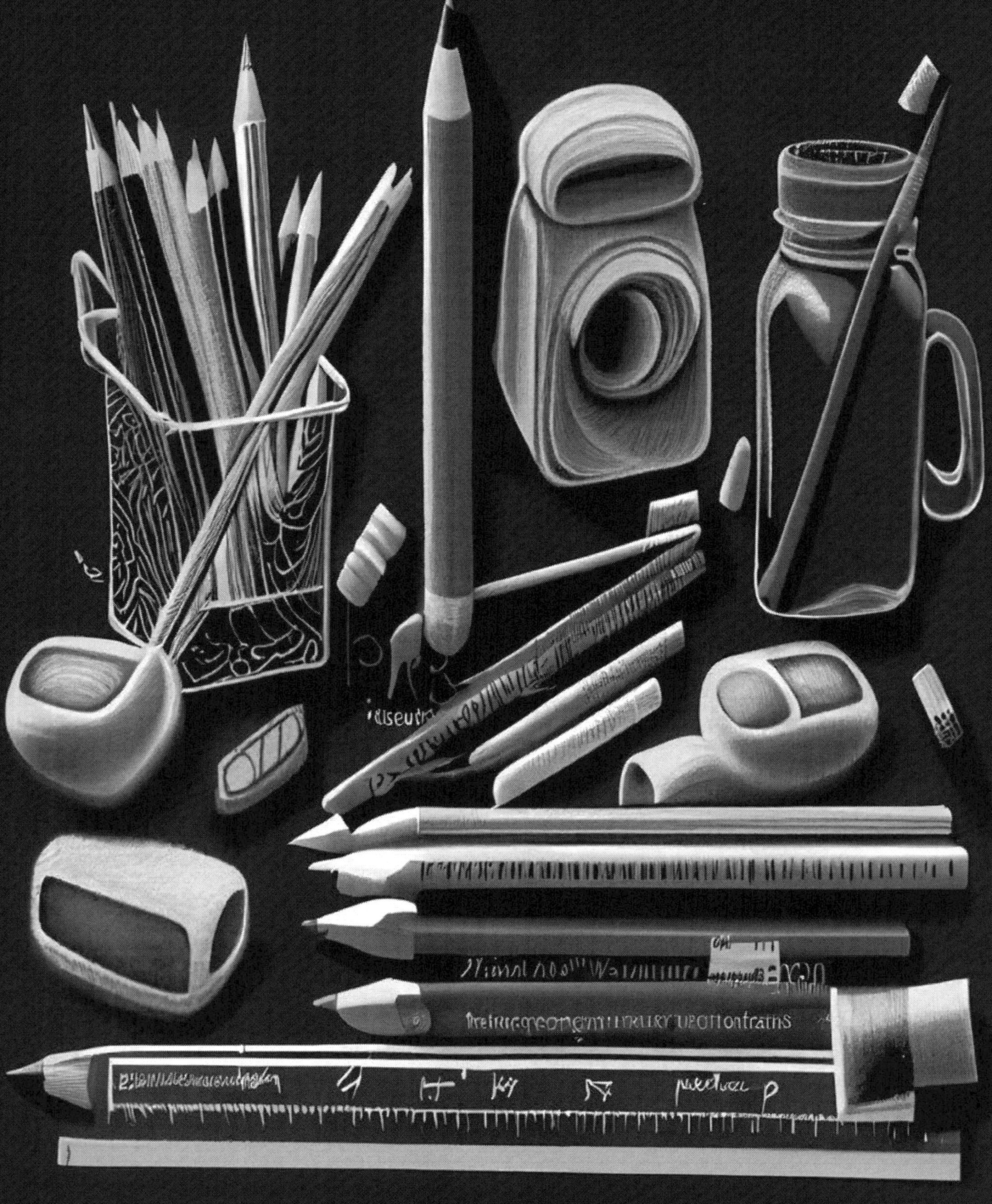

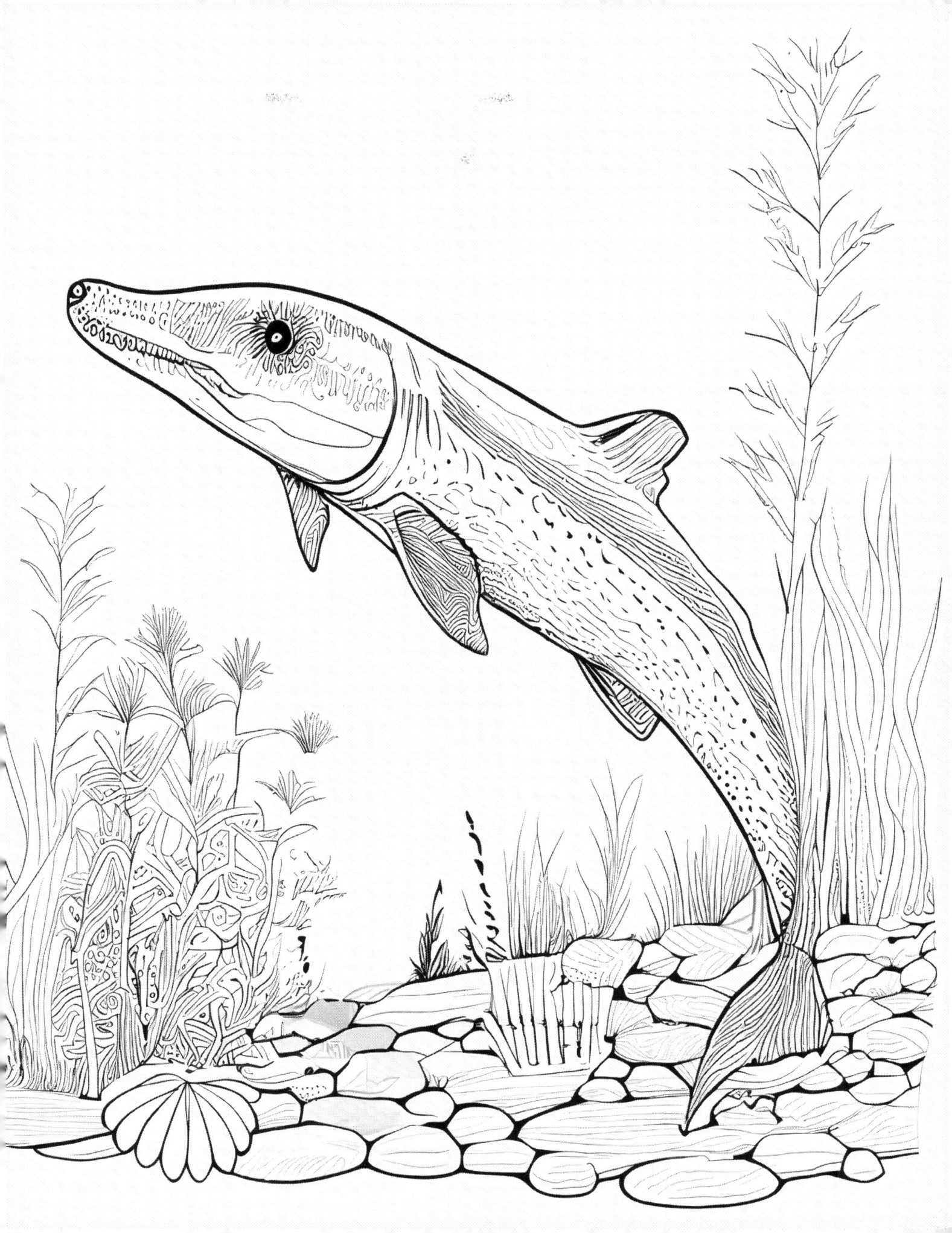

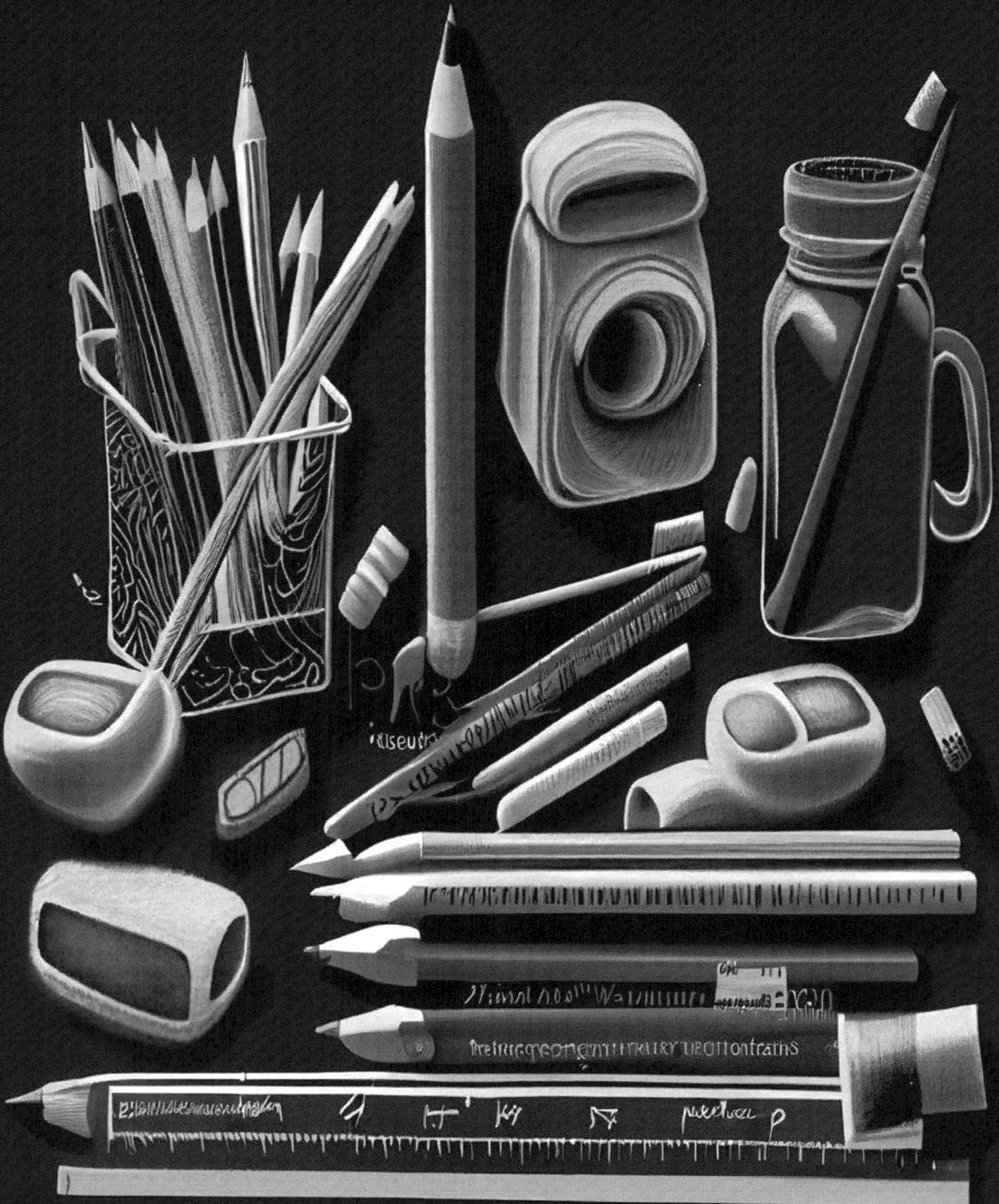

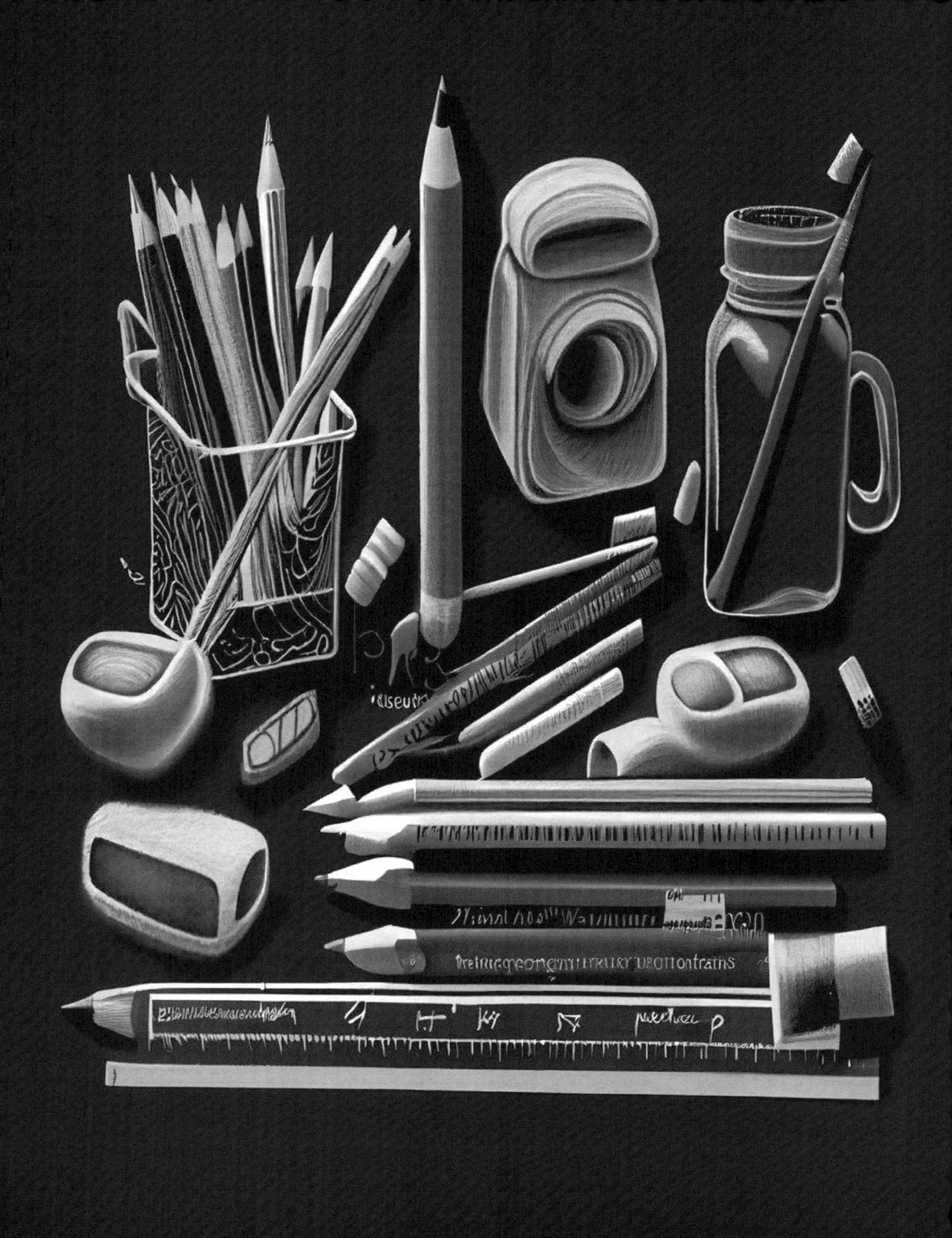

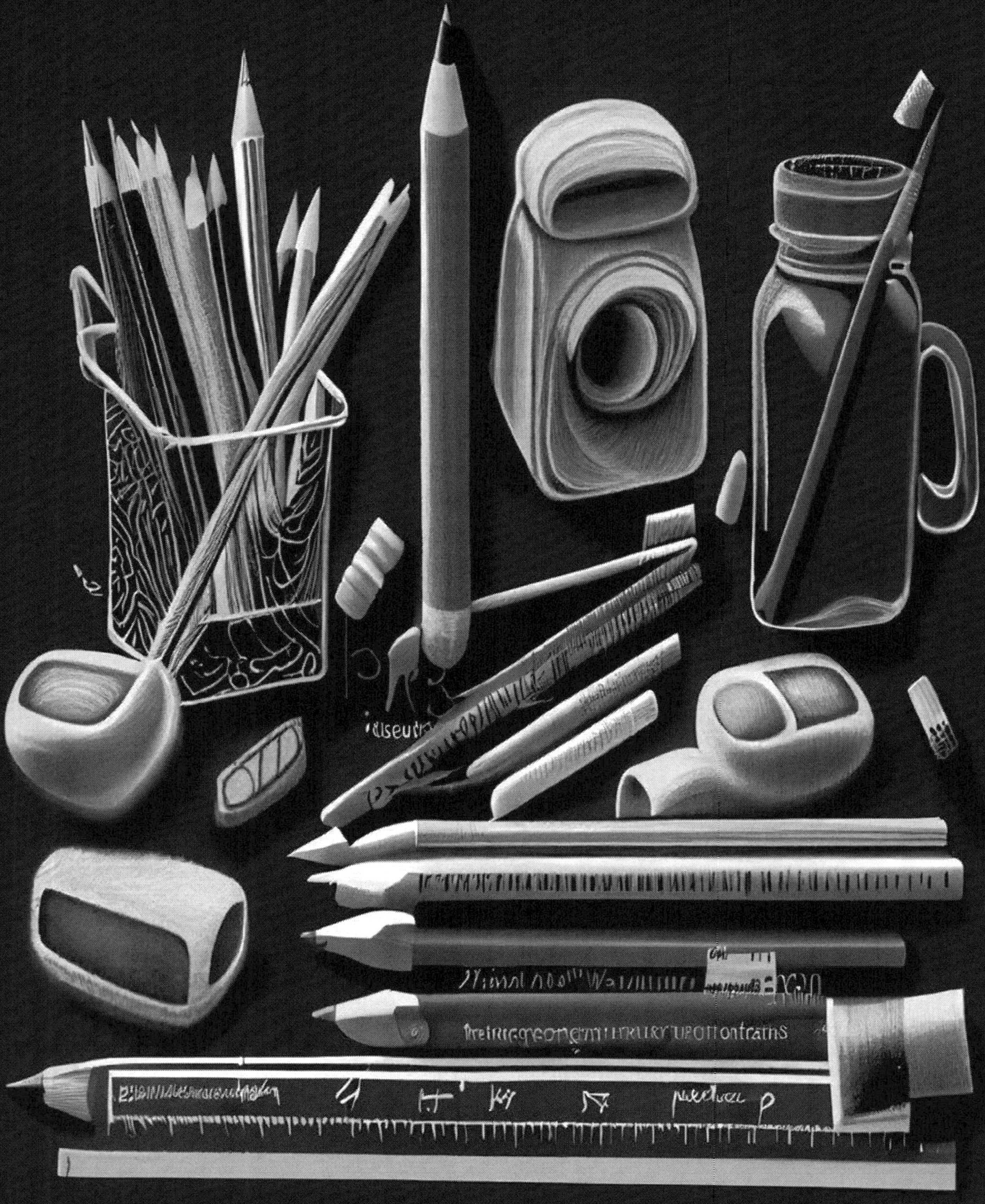

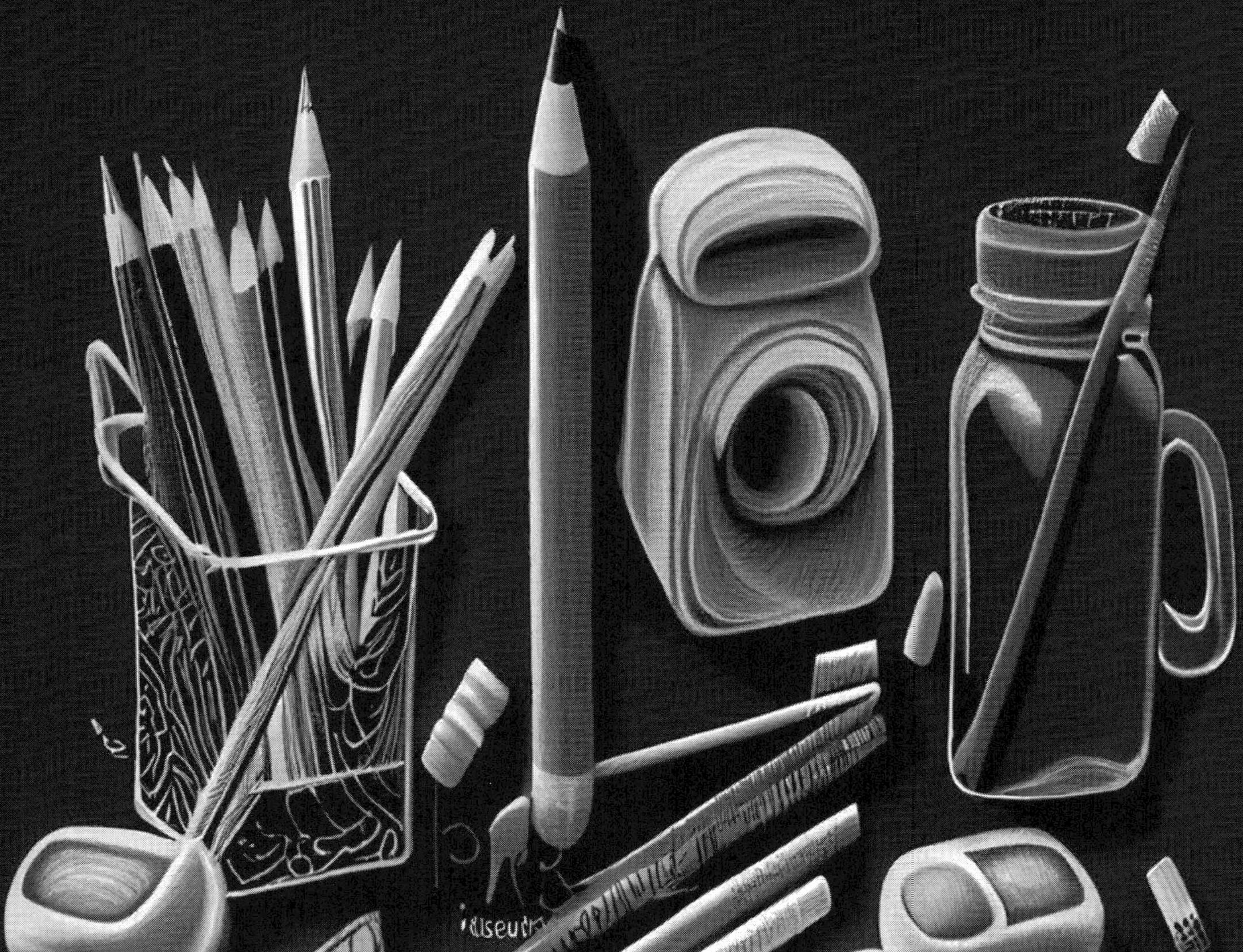

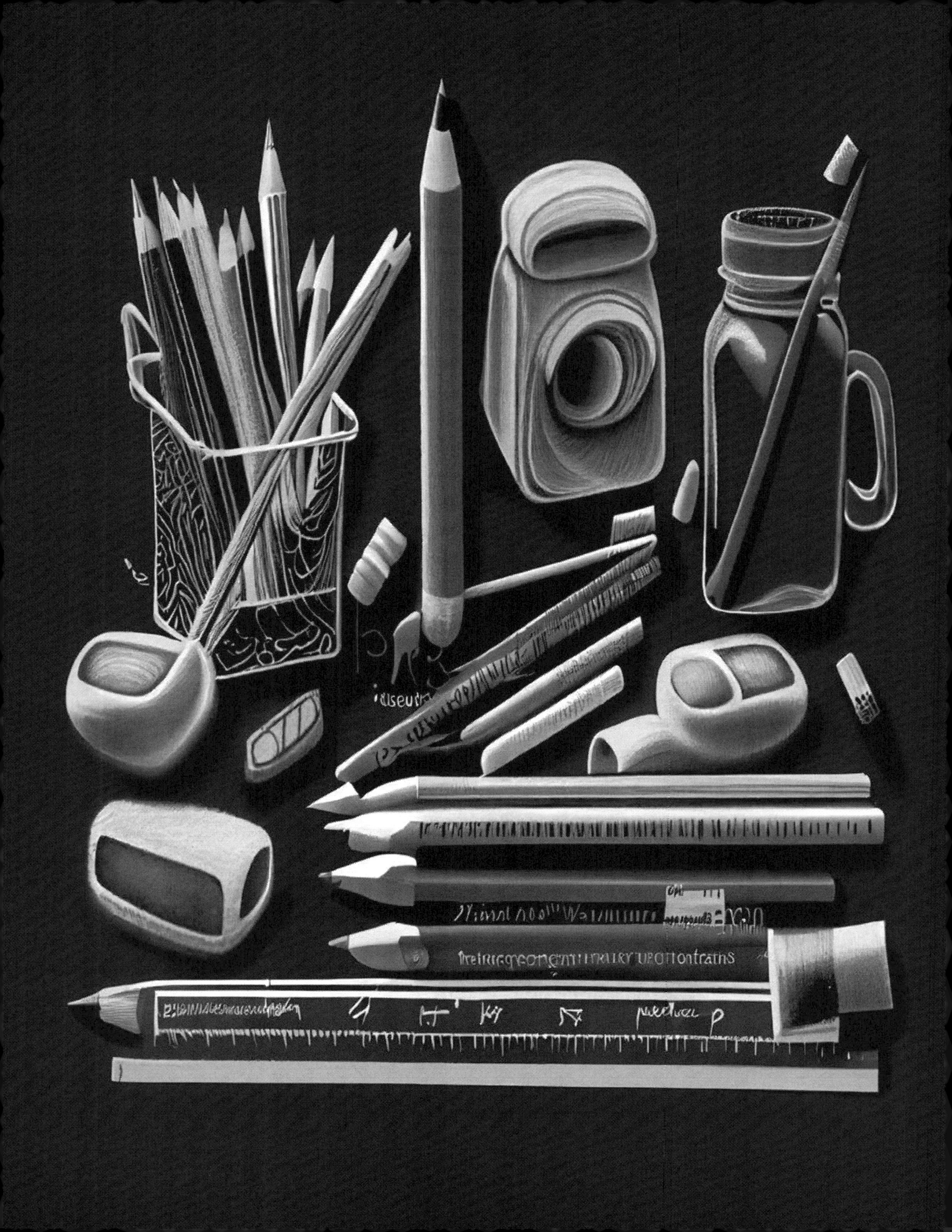

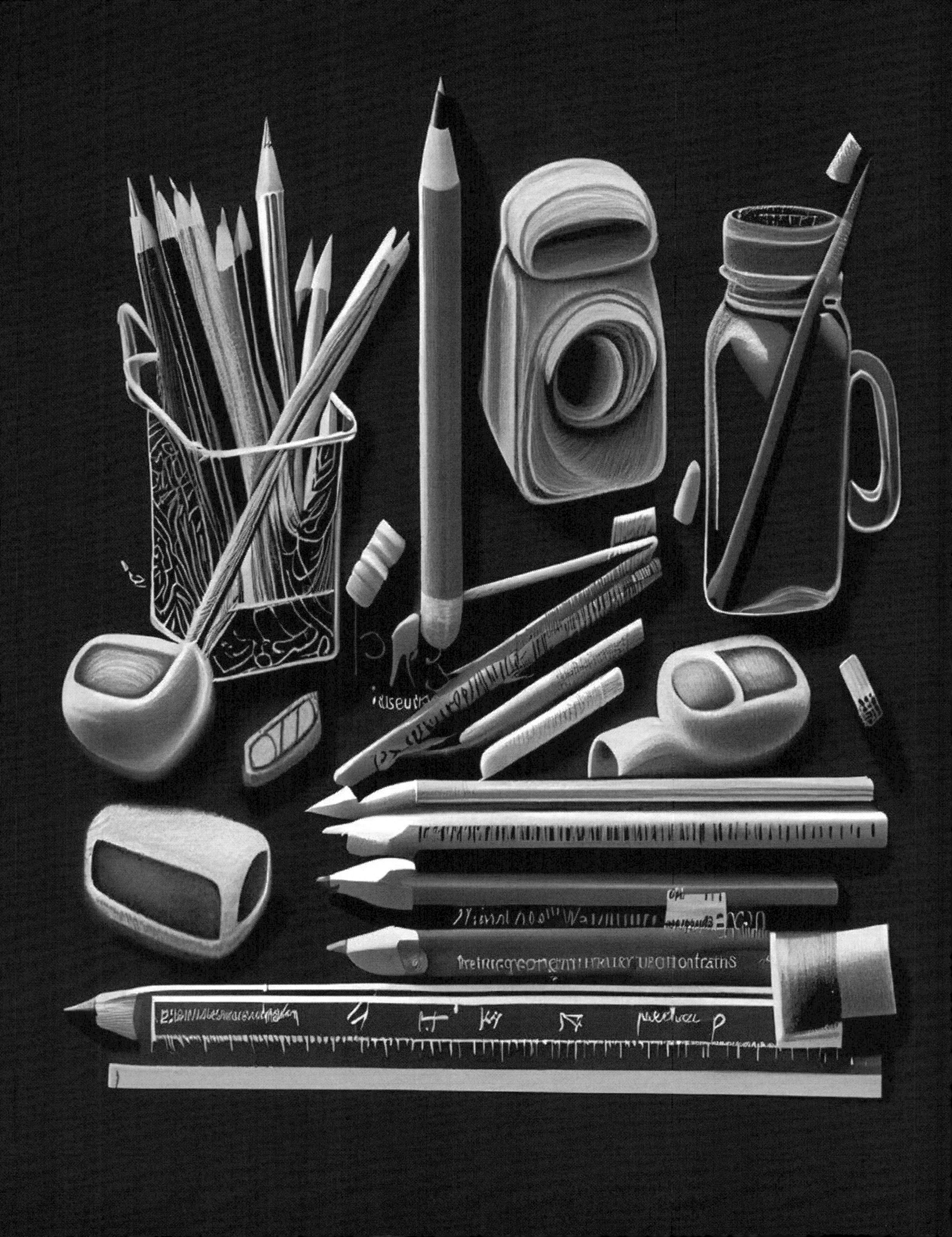

# Congratulations

Dear,

Thank you very much for choosing this coloring book. We are very grateful for the trust you have placed in our work and hope you have enjoyed the book.

If you have a few minutes, we would greatly appreciate it if you could leave a review on Amazon. Your opinion is very valuable and can help this book interest other people. Also, sharing your thoughts and opinions on what you liked most about the book and which drawings you found the most interesting can be useful for others.

Leaving a review on Amazon is a useful way to share your thoughts and opinions about the book with other buyers. In addition to sharing what you liked about the book, you can also mention any point that you believe could be improved. This can be useful for the author or editor and can help future buyers have a clearer idea of what they can expect from the book.

Warm regards,

Made in the USA
Las Vegas, NV
20 July 2023